THE Kids' BOOK OF QUESTIONS

D0950756

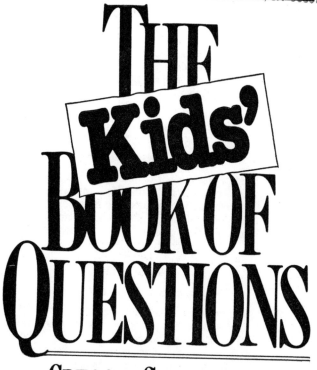

THE Kids' BOOK OF QUESTIONS

GREGORY STOCK, PH.D.

WORKMAN PUBLISHING, NEW YORK

Library of Congress Cataloging-in-Publication Data

Stock, Gregory.
The kids' book of questions.

Summary: Poses thought-provoking questions to the reader about such issues as trust, fear, ethics, family problems, social pressures, and friendship.
1. Children—Conduct of life—Miscellanea.
[1. Conduct of life—Miscellanea. 2. Questions and answers] I. Title.
BJ1631.S83   1988   170'.880544   88-40230
ISBN 0-89480-631-9 (pbk.)

Cover illustration: Tom Lulevitch

Workman books are available at special discounts when purchased in bulk for premiums and sales promotions as well as for fund-raising or educational use. Special editions or book excerpts can also be created to specification. For details, contact the Special Sales Director at the address below.

Workman Publishing Company, Inc.
708 Broadway
New York, NY 10003

Manufactured in the United States of America
First printing September 1988

20   19   18   17   16

To Stacie
for our early-morning walks
to snail heaven

To Katy
for her sharp eye for squad cars

And to the children in my future
for things I won't even try to guess

Nathaniel,
may you continue to ask questions
and search for the answers
that are right for you

—David

Acknowledgments

For their ideas, suggestions, and encouragement, I particularly thank Lillian McKinstry, Don Ponturo, and Billie Stock. I also thank Douglas Balfour, Joan Batson, Joseph Cambray, Kenny Cleveland, Sheila Garrigue, Jamie Haber, Jason Ide, Nettie Ide, Brenda Jackson, William Jackson, Rachel Parcel, Alby Segal, Nat Sinnwell, Katherine Stock, Jane Stock, Randi Zielinski, Jason Sullivan, Daniel Summer, Claudia Summer, Fred Weber, and the Denver Children's Museum.

For his expert editorial assistance as well as his many ideas and suggestions, I thank Michael Cader.

Finally, I thank David Breznau. Without his involvement with the original BOOK OF QUESTIONS this kids' book would not now exist.

Introduction

Most of the questions you are asked at school have right and wrong answers: Who invented the steam engine? What is the capital of Italy? How is blue cheese made? Since such questions have answers you can find in books, it is not all that important if you sometimes don't know their answers.

The questions here do not have answers you can find in books because they are about you. Knowing what you believe in and who you are is important, so look into yourself to find answers to these questions. This is not a test, though, and no one answer is right for everyone. Here, there are no correct answers—only honest ones—and you are the only one who really knows how honest you are being. Don't respond as you think others want you to; respond the way you actually feel.

THE KIDS' BOOK OF QUESTIONS is for kids, but it is not a book of childish questions. Some questions are playful and even downright silly; others are serious and focus upon the hard dilemmas you face in growing up. They raise issues such as dealing with authority, understanding friendship, handling social pressures, overcoming fears, and deciding what's right and wrong. You will face these issues, in one form or another, throughout your life.

Growing up is not easy these days. Kids are not sheltered from divorce, crime, drugs, sex, and many other things that are hard even for adults to deal with. You get a lot of advice from your parents, from your friends, from your teachers, and even from television; but often different people say different things about what you should and shouldn't do. What is right? Where do you fit into the world? Who can you trust? A big part of growing up is learning to decide such things for yourself.

Thinking about questions like the ones in

this book is a good way of learning to do just that. When you use your imagination to explore difficult dilemmas, you can learn from things without going through them in real life. So throw yourself wholeheartedly into these questions and pretend they are real. When you really care about the decisions you make, you will discover many new ideas and opinions that are entirely your own. Take this chance to discuss some things you feel strongly about instead of everyday things you've talked about dozens of times before.

With some of these questions you will pretend you have extraordinary powers or are in extraordinary situations. With others, you will remember your past or imagine your future. Treat these questions as your own. Play with them, add to them, change them, but don't cheat by trying to figure out ways to avoid having to make difficult choices. And please, don't just answer yes or no—or let others get away with that. Try to explore why you and your friends feel the way you do; you'll find that the reasons behind people's answers are even more interesting than the answers themselves.

Playing with questions of this sort is a game to laugh and have fun with. It is also, at times, a little uncomfortable for it is not always easy to look at what kind of person you are, what you want, and what you care about. Talking about your thoughts and feelings with your friends will be a big help not only when you come to difficult and confusing questions in this book, but also when you next face some tough choices in your own life. At those times, remember that growing occurs not from having answers but from searching for answers.

A big difference between questions about things and questions about people is that with personal questions you are never quite sure where they will lead. Maybe that is why personal questions are so much fun. This book gives you an easy and a playful way of raising some issues you've wanted to talk about but haven't known how to bring up. You can use these questions by yourself, with your friends, or even with adults.

Start asking the questions you find here, and similar questions of your own, and you'll soon be having some lively discussions. I hope THE KIDS' BOOK OF QUESTIONS helps you see how rewarding it can be to ask thought-provoking questions. It is often quite amazing to find out where one little question can lead you. Good luck and have fun.

THE
Kids'
BOOK OF
QUESTIONS

1

If you were the ruler of the world and you could have anything you wanted as well as have people do anything you wanted, do you think you would get greedy and mean or would you be a good and fair ruler?

2

Do you think boys or girls have it easier?

3

If your mother promised to be home at 2:00 in the afternoon to take you to the movies but didn't show up until suppertime and didn't even phone, what would be a good punishment for her? Would punishing her be likely to make her on time in the future?

4

If all your best friends were willing to be absolutely honest and tell you exactly what they liked most about you and what they liked least about you, would you want them to?

5

Would you rather have a strict teacher who was fair and taught well or a teacher who was relaxed and fun but didn't teach very well?

6

One day your father gets a really weird idea and dyes his hair green. Knowing everyone would be looking at him and snickering, would you go to the shopping center with him if he wanted your company?

7

When you make a mistake, do you make up excuses? If so, do you think people believe you?

8

If you could have a round-trip ride in a time machine and travel any distance into the past or future, where would you want to go?

9

If a friend had an important secret and didn't want other people to learn about it, would telling you the secret be a big mistake?

10

If your parents were worried about a serious problem that had nothing to do with you directly, would you want them to tell you about it or would you rather not know?

11

What would you do if everyone in your family forgot your birthday?

12

How would you act differently if you had a younger sister who idolized you and tried to copy everything you did? What things do you think your parents do only because they want to set an example for you?

13

If you were alone and had only a few minutes to hide from crooks who were about to break into your house, where would you hide? What is the best hiding place in your house?

14

Do you think you have too many chores? If you could assign the chores in your house, which ones would you take for yourself?

15

Some adults have a lot of trouble enjoying themselves. If you were asked to give them some advice about how to play and have more fun, what would you say?

16

Who do you dislike the most? What is the best thing about that person?

17

Do you sometimes find yourself sitting in front of some awful-tasting food you have been told you have to eat? If so, what is your best trick for getting rid of it without getting caught?

18

If you could be invisible for a day, what would you do?

19

When did you get yourself in the biggest mess by telling a lie? What do you think would have happened if you had just told the truth?

20

If you could choose any bedtime you wanted for the next year, what time would you pick?

21

Are there things you pretend not to like but really do enjoy—for example, being kissed by your parents or having a little sister tag along with you? If so, why do you hide your feelings?

22

When you are mad at your parents and want to get back at them, what little things do you do to anger or embarrass them?

23

If you had to guess two things you will like in a few years but don't like now, what would you guess? Pretend that if you are correct you will win $1,000.

24

If you had the choice of maturing physically and sexually a full year before any of your friends or at about the same time as the rest of your friends, which would you choose? Why?

25

If you knew that by being the teacher's pet for two years you would lose all your friends and be teased by everyone, but that you would later grow to be very successful and happy, would you do it?

26

Would you like to have an identical twin? What about it would be best? worst?

27

Would you rather your father gave you more presents or spent more time with you? Which would make you feel he loved you more?

28

If you were offered $100 to kiss someone you liked in front of your school class, would you do it?

What is the worst nightmare you can re-member? Would you be willing to have the same dream tonight if it meant you could spend a weekend in Disneyland?

30

If you woke up tomorrow and by magic were already grown-up and had kids of your own, how would you treat them differently from the way your parents treat you?

31

How would you feel if you found out today you were adopted when you were a baby? Would you try to find your natural parents?

32

If you agreed to sell your bike to a friend and then someone offered you more money, would you go back on the bargain?

33

If you and your friends were collecting money for a charity, and then your friends decided to steal what they were collecting and said they wouldn't be friends with you anymore unless you did it too, what would you do?

34

If you could be as talented as some friend of yours at any one thing, what would you choose?

35

Would you rather pick what you wear to school or wear the same uniform every day? What would you wear if no one paid any attention to the way you dressed?

36

Clean your room! Take a bath! Wash your hands! Why do you think adults care so much about cleanliness?

37

If you told your friends everything about yourself, including the things you are most ashamed and afraid of, do you think they would like you less or more than they do now?

38

Are you in a hurry to grow up? What does it mean to be "grown-up," and when do you think it will happen to you?

39

While on vacation you get a ride to the beach with a friend's parents and find that some people are bathing nude. Would you want to stay and watch or leave?

40

If people stopped growing and getting stronger by the time they reached your age, and so adults were neither bigger nor stronger than you are, would you still do what they said? If so, why?

41

If you had only five minutes to think up a nickname for yourself and knew everyone would use it for years, what would you pick? What would you pick for your best friend? your parents?

42

Imagine that your principal told you she wanted to make school better and would change it in any one way you suggested. What would you tell her to do?

43

Of all the things you have been told about God and about religion, what do you think is true and what do you think isn't?

44

If you could permanently trade lives with one of your brothers, sisters, or classmates, would you? If so, who would you pick and why?

45

If you could change any one thing about your parents, what would it be?

46

What things do you think children should be punished for, and how should it be done? Is there an age when people are too old to be punished for the mistakes they make? If so, what age and why?

47

What are you most proud of having done?
What would make you even more proud?

48

If you were certain that everyone in your class but you would be killed unless you agreed to die in their place, would you save everyone else or save yourself? Would it matter if no one would ever know about what you had done?

49

What do you like most about your best friend? How long do you think it would take to make another "best" friend if you moved to a distant city and could never see the best friend you have now?

50

Would you rather be very poor and have parents who loved you and each other, or be wealthy and have parents who ignored you and were always fighting with each other?

51

If someone pulled down a friend's pants at a movie theater, would you join in the laughter?

52

What is the most boring thing you can imagine doing? Would you do it for a whole week if you could then celebrate your birthday twice each year?

53

What is the biggest difference between what happens on television and what happens in the real world?

54

Are there people you trust so much you wouldn't be afraid to have them know your every thought?

55

Would you be willing to never again get any gifts and surprises if instead you could just ask for anything you wanted and have your parents buy it for you?

56

What makes you feel guilty? Do people try to make you feel guilty very often?

57

If someone a lot smaller than you kept teasing you and telling lies about you and wouldn't stop, how far would you be willing to go to make the person stop? What about someone bigger than you?

58

Have you ever thought you were going to die—for example, in a big thunderstorm or an accident? If so, how did it feel and is there anything you learned from the experience that you could tell your friends?

59

When was the last time you were so mad at a friend that you screamed? Do you think you get over your anger more quickly when you show how mad you are or when you hide it?

60

Which subjects at school do you think will be completely useless to you in the future? Which ones do you think will be important to you?

61

If you knew no harm would come to you, would you be willing to spend two days alone inside your home? Pretend you could have any present you wanted if you did it.

62

When was the last time you told your parents you loved them?

63

Are there certain kinds of stealing—or borrowing without permission—that are all right and others that are not? If so, how would you explain the difference? When was the last time you stole something or thought about doing so?

64

What is the hardest thing about growing up?

65

When someone says you are just like your mom or your dad, do you like it? Do you try more to be like your parents or to be different from them?

66

Would you rather hang around with a group of younger kids and be the boss but do things that younger kids do, or hang around with a group of older kids and be the squirt but do things that older kids get to do?

67

What was the most exciting thing you ever did on a dare? Are you glad you did it?

68

Would you eat a worm sandwich if doing so meant that next week you could appear on your favorite TV show?

69

Would you like your parents to touch, cuddle, and hug each other more or less than they do now? What about having them touch and hug you more or less often?

'70

If you found a change purse on the playground with quite a bit of money in it and no one saw you pick it up, what would you do?

71

Is there any argument you have again and again with your parents? If so, what do you think you could do to prevent it? Do you sometimes just enjoy arguing?

72

What was the luckiest thing that ever happened to you?

73

If you liked someone who later turned out to be a liar, would you still want to be good friends?

74

What advice would you give if someone's mom and dad were getting divorced and they were always trying to make him take sides in their arguments? Imagine that he loves both his parents equally.

'75

Did you ever stand up for something you thought was right even though a lot of people got upset with you? If not, do you think you would ever be strong enough to do so?

'76

Do you act like different people when you are with your friends, your family, and your schoolmates?

77

What sorts of things are too personal to discuss with your parents? Is there anyone you could discuss those things with?

78

Do you have many mementos and souvenirs? If so, how much money would someone have to give you to get you to throw them all away?

79

What is something you love doing now but will probably not enjoy in two years?

80

On Halloween, a group of high-school students are caught scaring little kids and stealing their candy. If you could decide the punishment, what would it be?

81

Would you rather be a rich and famous movie star or a great doctor who saves a lot of people but is not wealthy or well known?

82

Have you ever seen your parents drunk or very ill? How did it feel to see them that way?

83

Of all the nice things someone could truthfully say about you, which one would make you feel the best?

84

What is the worst word you know? How did you learn it and when was the last time you said it?

85

When is the last time you really laughed at yourself because you did something silly or stupid?

86

If you could have some friend be your slave for a day and do anything you wanted, what would you ask for? Pretend your friend wouldn't get upset no matter what you wanted.

87

If you could make your parents try any one food, what would it be? Do you think children should be forced to try new foods?

88

If this Saturday you could do absolutely anything you wanted, what would you do?

89

Who are your heroes? Why do you think they are so terrific?

90

When was the last time you lied to your parents? to a close friend? When was the last time you got caught lying?

91

What tricks do your friends use to get you to do things they know you really don't want to do?

92

Do you pick your nose or bite your nails? If so, do you think you always will, or will you stop one day?

93

What things have adults told you that you suspect are not really true? Do you think they actually believe those things?

94

If you could change any one thing about the way you look, what would it be?

95

If your favorite pet needed an expensive operation and could have it only if you agreed that the operation would replace your Christmas and birthday presents for the next two years, would you go along with it?

96

Are you afraid to ask questions when you don't understand something? For example, do you sometimes fake a laugh when you don't understand a joke?

97

What is the best costume you ever wore? Would you like getting dressed up in costumes once every week instead of just a few times a year?

98

Have you and your friends ever picked on people and made fun of them until they cried? If so, why did you do it? Did you enjoy it?

99

Are there things your parents won't do themselves, but still make you do because it's "good for you"? If so, do you feel this is fair?

100

If an older kid hit you, stole something of yours, and then told you he'd hurt you if you told on him, would you tell anyone? If so, who?

101

Are you more likely to hold back your tears when you feel like crying or to hold back your laughter when you see something funny? Why?

102

Do you wish your parents would question you less or more about what you do and how you feel?

103

If your parents told you your best friend was a bad influence on you and that you were no longer allowed to play together, how would you feel? Would you do what they said?

104

Have you ever farted and then blamed someone else?

105

If you knew you wouldn't get caught, would you cheat on a test by copying someone's answers? What would you think if you saw other people cheating?

106

When was the last time you were generous to a stranger just because you wanted to be nice?

107

If you knew it would save the lives of ten starving children in another country, would you be willing to go without any new clothes for the next year? What about having bad acne for a year?

108

If a good friend did something bad and you were asked if you knew anything about it, would you lie to keep your friend from getting into trouble?

109

If you knew that by practicing hard every Saturday you could become the best in your school at whatever you wanted, what—if anything—would you work on? Now imagine looking back on your choice in twenty years; do you think you would wish you had picked something else to work on?

110

What is your biggest fear? How would your life be different if suddenly you overcame it?

111

If your parents lost their jobs and you had to try to help support your family, what sorts of things would you do to earn money?

112

If you could pick any one food and have as much of it as you wanted—but nothing else—during the next week, what would you pick?

113

What would make you try harder in school: wanting to please a teacher you liked a lot? not wanting to disappoint your parents? being offered a fabulous prize if you did well?

114

How important is it for you to win? When was the last time you cheated in a game so you could win?

115

If you got so angry at your parents that you decided to run away, where would you go? If you ran away, do you think you would ever come home again?

116

If there were a hard but exciting project to do, would you rather do it by yourself and get all the credit for it, or do it with a group of friends knowing that everyone would share the credit? What would it feel like to do it the other way?

117

What was the most embarrassing thing that ever happened to you? Are you embarrassed now by the same things that used to embarrass you?

118

Whose room would you most like to spend the afternoon looking through? Pretend you had permission to look at all the private possessions of that person.

119

If you had the choice of either being confined to your room for two days or being spanked, which would you choose? Why?

120

Do your parents try to trick you into doing things they want you to do? If so, do you usually figure out what's going on right away or not until later?

121

If you could grow up to be famous and successful, what would you like to be known for? Do you think you will be famous one day?

122

If you had to either always rush and do things a lot more quickly than you do now, or always take your time and do things a lot more slowly than you do now, which would you prefer? Does it bother you to be around people who are quite a bit faster or slower than you?

123

If you could do one thing you are not allowed to do now because you are too young, what would you pick?

124

When were you last in a fight? What things would you be willing to fight about even though they don't directly threaten you?

125

If you could be either the most attractive, the most athletic, or the smartest kid in your class, which would you choose?

126

What do you think your parents worried about when they were your age? What do you think they worry about now?

127

If you were to be granted any one magical power you wanted, what would you pick?

128

If you liked your uncle a lot, and if one day when you were alone together he tried to touch you in a way that felt wrong to you, would you tell someone, try to pretend it hadn't happened, try to avoid him, or do something else? What would you do if the same thing happened again?

129

If, by wishing it, you could have every person in the world wake up and have the same skin color, would you want that to happen?

130

If you could have a wonderful new experience you could cherish or a great new possession, which would you want? Why?

131

Would you rather see all sex or all violence censored from television? Why?

132

What kinds of teasing do you think you would miss most if everyone decided to never tease you again?

133

What do you think your friends like most about you? If you lost that quality, do you think they would still like you?

134

Adults can do more but have more responsibilities; children can play more but are often told what to do. Do you think kids or adults have a better deal?

135

If you could make a TV show about anything you wanted and you knew that millions of people would see it, what would it be about?

136

Would you rather have a job you didn't like that paid a lot or a job you loved that paid just enough to get by on?

137

If you could see into the future but not change it, would you want to do so?

138

What is the wildest and craziest thing you've ever done? Would you like to do it again?

139

Have you ever gotten yourself into a mess by telling people you could do things you really couldn't do?

140

If your two best friends got so mad at each other that they both refused to come to your birthday party if the other were there, what would you do?

141

If you were mad at your brother and found out about something bad he had done, would you tell your parents so that he'd get into trouble?

142

Imagine you got hit by a car and could be saved only by a special operation. The operation would give you a normal, happy life, but would unfortunately cause you fifteen minutes of terrible, stabbing pain every morning when you awoke. Would you want to have the operation?

143

If one morning you woke up and found that during the night you had been magically changed into an adult, what would you do? Pretend you know you will become a kid again in one week.

144

If your big brother offered you some drugs,
what would you do?

145

How many different people do you think it
is possible to love at one time? Why?

146

If you couldn't watch TV for a year, what do you think you would do with all of your extra time? Do you think you would be better off if you watched TV more or less than you do now? Why?

147

Are you worried about what kind of place the world will be when you grow up? If so, what worries you most and what do you think could be done to improve things?

148

If you knew that by cheating you could win an important competition for your school and be a hero, would you? Pretend you were sure you wouldn't get caught.

149

If you could have either the ability to talk to animals or the power to see into the future, which would you want?

150

If you could have anyone you know as a best friend, who would you pick?

151

If everyone in your class began teasing and picking on your best friend, and you knew that if you stayed friends everyone would start picking on you, would you stay friends?

152

How would it make you feel if most people thought you were two years younger than you are? two years older?

153

What do you feel your parents should do for you or give to you without even expecting to be thanked—for example, cooking meals, buying clothes, or taking you places? Do you think they feel you don't need to thank them for these things?

154

Have you had any personal experiences that lead you to believe in God? If so, why do you think there are so many people who haven't had such experiences? If not, why do you think so many other people have had them?

155

What is the best trick you ever played on someone?

156

Who do you think are our country's ene-
mies? What exactly do you think they
would do to you if they became the rulers
here?

157

If your parents didn't care whether you got good grades or not, would you be upset? What is something you know more about than the kid who gets the best grades in your class?

158

What advice would you give to a good friend who got very jealous of someone and started trying to act just like that person?

159

At what age should kids be able to wear whatever they want to school? At what age should they be allowed to date?

160

What mark would you give your teacher for her overall performance? for her patience? for her friendliness? for her handwriting?

161

How do you feel when you see someone who is disfigured or crippled? Could you be best friends with someone who was extremely ugly?

162

Why do you think the most popular kids in school are so popular? In what ways do you think you are better than they are?

163

Is there anything so bad that if you found out your mother had done it, you would turn her in to the police?

164

Do you try to act like your friends more than they try to act like you? Why?

165

Do you usually say what you really think or what you believe people want to hear?

166

Pretend you can own only one pair of shoes and have to choose between a pair that looks funny but feels great and another pair that looks terrific but feels lousy. Which would you pick?

167

If a rich kid wanted to buy your parents, how much would you ask for them—assuming you were willing to sell? Would you trade parents with any of your friends?

168

What is the best birthday party you can imagine having?

169

If you were riding your bicycle and ran into someone else's bike and wrecked it—but no one saw you—what would you do?

170

Have you ever been humiliated by a teacher? If so, what happened?

171

Would you rather regularly wet your bed and have only your parents know about it or never wet your bed but, because of a story someone made up about you, have everyone think you did?

172

Would it be worse to spend one night all alone in an empty house in the woods, or to spend it with a friend outdoors in a violent thunderstorm?

173

If you were told you could give a ten-minute speech to your school on any subject you chose, would you want to do so?

174

What things that you were afraid of a few years ago no longer disturb you?

175

If you were given $1,000 to use to help other people, how would you spend it?

176

Would you rather have more brothers and sisters than you have now or fewer? What do you think is the best size for a family? Why?

177

Do you think that when you grow up your parents will feel you did better than they had hoped you would do or not as well?

178

Of all the things you could imagine doing when you grow up, which one would most please your parents? most disappoint them?

179

Would you rather your family loved one another and always showed how they felt— sometimes fighting and yelling, sometimes hugging and kissing—or would you prefer they loved one another and hid their feelings whenever they were upset or angry?

180

If you could have your room either clean and neat all the time or jumbled and messy, which would you prefer?

181

What things scare you even though you know there is no reason to be afraid?

182

Have you ever—without telling anyone—let someone beat you at a game you could easily have won? If so, why?

183

Can you remember a time you succeeded in doing something you thought you would never be able to do? If so, how did it feel? Would you rather try more ambitious things knowing you might fail, or try easier things knowing you would be sure to succeed?

184

If you had to pick an age to be for your whole life, knowing that you would just stay at that age and never grow older, what age would you pick?

185

If you were a teacher and the kids in your class wouldn't listen to you, what would you do? What if you did that and they still wouldn't listen?

186

Do you think kids should not be allowed to watch certain movies and TV shows? If so, what sorts of things shouldn't they be permitted to see?

187

If you could live someone else's life for a week—just to see what it would be like—would you want to? If so, who would you pick and why?

188

Imagine a good friend came in with a black eye one day and at first wouldn't say how it happened, but later—when you promised not to tell anyone—confessed that his father had gotten mad and hit him. Would you try to do anything to help him? What if two months later the same thing happened again?

189

When was the last time you felt completely happy? What made you feel that way?

190

If your babysitter said she'd let you stay up way past your bedtime if you promised not to tell your parents—no matter what—would you agree? If you agreed, what would you say if the next morning your mother asked you if you had gone to bed on time?

191

What was the worst accident you ever caused? Were you angrier at yourself than other people were, or was it the other way around?

192

What is your favorite daydream?

193

Have you ever been blamed for something you didn't do, yet not told on the person who really did it? If so, why didn't you tell?

194

Which would be worse: not watching TV for a month or having to come straight home and stay in the house every day for a month?

195

What are the stupidest rules your parents have about what you can't do or must do?

196

If for one day you could do absolutely anything you wanted and not get caught or punished, what would you do?

197

If you had to pick a new first name for yourself, what would you choose?

198

If eating nothing but a tasteless food paste for a year would make you a lot stronger and more attractive, would you do it?

199

If a friend gave you a gift you didn't like, would you act as though you really did like it?

200

Who is the meanest person to kids in your neighborhood? If you were sure you wouldn't get caught, what trick would you play on him on Halloween? If you had to make up a story about how that person became so mean, what would it be?

201

What was your biggest failure?

202

If a friend threw a party and didn't invite you, what would you do?

203

Would you rather be the tallest person in your class or be just average in height?

204

What do you think your family would miss the most about you if you were to die? What would you miss most about them if they died?

205

Do you believe in God? If not, why do you think so many people believe in God? If so, what do you think God does all day?

206

If you could set your own allowance, how much would it be? How did you decide on that amount?

207

After being given a truth pill, you are asked to describe your family. What would you say?

208

If you could gaze into a magic mirror and see exactly what is happening anywhere in the world, where would you look and what do you think you would see?

209

If your teacher and your mother spent an afternoon discussing you, would you like to be able to hear what they were saying? What do you think they would say?

210

Have you ever wished someone were dead—or at least had very bad luck? If so, who and why?

211

Would you rather have to repeat a grade in school or gain a lot of weight?

212

Have you ever seen your mother or father cry? If not, how do you think it would feel to see that?

213

What, if anything, really gets on your nerves?

214

What would be the best thing that could happen to you? the worst thing?

215

What is the thing you dislike most about yourself? Do you think other people care about it as much as you do?

216

When you and your friends play together, do you prefer being at your house or at theirs? Why?

217

If you were to be stranded for ten years on a tiny island paradise about the size of a football field, how many people would you want with you and who would they be? Make believe you would be in no danger and would have a place to sleep as well as any food you needed.

218

What things do you see people doing just to fill up time and keep themselves busy? What things do you do for that same reason?

219

If you could be a rich and famous rock star but would have to dress strangely and bite the heads off frogs on stage, would you do it?

220

Who do you like the most? What is the worst thing about that person?

221

Would you rather change out of a wet bathing suit in a crowded public locker room, or wait until you could change in private when you got home an hour later?

222

If you were allowed to stop going to school, would you? What is the worst thing about school? the best?

223

Do you think it is fun to be a parent? If so, what do you think is the best thing about it? If not, why do you think people have children?

224

If you were to offer your parents one tip on how they could be better parents, what would you tell them?

225

What is the bravest thing you ever did?

226

If you became so sick that you would die if you didn't stay hooked up to a large life-support machine for the rest of your life, would you want someone to pull the plug?

227

If you bought something in a store and the clerk gave you a dollar extra in change, would you say anything about his mistake?

228

If something happened to your parents and you had to live with someone else for two years, who would you most like to be with?

229

What question would you be afraid to ask someone because of the answer you might get?

230

If a teacher really wanted to find out what you thought and felt, how could she best go about getting to know you?

231

Do adults sometimes try to get you to watch TV so you won't bother them? If so, how does that make you feel? Would you ever do something similar with kids you had to watch?

232

If a friend's mother died, what would you say to try to help comfort your friend? What could you tell your friend about death?

233

How do you think your life would be different if you were three inches taller? three inches shorter?

234

Would you lie to protect a good friend if you knew he had stolen something from a neighbor and your father asked you what you knew about it?

235

Would you be embarrassed to cry in front of your friends? your father? your little sister? If so, which would be worse and why?

236

If next year you could go to any school you chose, would you want to go somewhere different? If so, in what way do you think it would be better?

237

If some friends of your parents served you some food you thought tasted disgusting and then asked you how you liked it, what would you say? Would your parents want you to tell the truth?

238

How do you think life would change for you if someone in your family became very ill and had to stay in a hospital for a long time?

239

If you had a lot of money and could use it in any way you wanted, what would you do with it?

240

Pretend there are three people in a doctor's office: a one-year-old baby, a grandmother with a lot of grandchildren who love her, and a teenager who works hard but just flunked out of high school. They are all seriously ill but you can save one of them. Which would you pick?

241

What do your parents do that embarrasses you the most?

242

What foreign country have you heard the most about? What do you think it would be like to grow up there?

243

What is one of your best tricks for getting attention from your parents? from your friends?

244

Would you like to have a brother who was just about the best brother you could imagine—friendly, smart, good at everything he tried, and close to you—if it meant that everyone would always talk about how great he was and not pay much attention to you?

245

Would you rather be slender and athletic but rather dumb, or fat and clumsy but very smart?

246

Would you rather receive a gift you really wanted, or give your mother a gift she would absolutely treasure?

247

Are you afraid there will be a nuclear war? If so, do you have any ideas about how to keep it from happening?

248

Would you rather have no rules at all or live with the rules you have now? If there weren't any rules, what would you do differently?

249

If someone is doing something that is wrong, is it usually better to tell an adult or to try to solve the problem on your own? For example, if you saw someone stealing things from other kids, would you tell a teacher? What if a big kid spit on your lunch?

250

If you knew that by never again eating junk foods or candy, you would live until age 75 rather than 60, would you give them up?

251

Do you think it would be worse to be raised by two parents who fought all the time but who both loved you, or by a single parent who loved you?

252

If you could decide right now whether or not you will smoke cigarettes when you grow up, what would you decide? What about using drugs, or drinking a lot? How do you think it would change your life if you did the opposite?

253

When was the last time you laughed so hard you cried? If you could watch a movie that was so funny it made you laugh that hard for two whole hours, would you want to?

254

What is the most unfair thing about the way your family is run?

255

If, by magic, you had the power to pick one person and always be able to read that person's mind, who would you pick?

256

What is the most important thing you have learned about life in the past few years? How did you learn it?

257

What is the funniest story you ever made up about why you weren't able to get your homework finished on time?

258

If drinking a magic potion would make you never again feel sad—no matter what happened—would you drink it?

259

Make believe that right now you have to pick the job you will have as an adult. What is the best job you can think of? What is the worst?

260

If you could ask your parents any questions for an hour and know they would tell you the absolute truth, what sorts of things would you ask? Pretend they would answer everything but afterward would forget they had even talked to you.

GREGORY STOCK first started asking questions as a child and has continued to do so as the author of several books, including the best-selling BOOK OF QUESTIONS, which has been translated into fifteen languages. He received a doctorate in biophysics from the Johns Hopkins University in 1977, and has published numerous papers in biophysics and developmental biology. A Baker Scholar, he received an MBA from the Harvard Business School in 1987.